Curriculum Visions

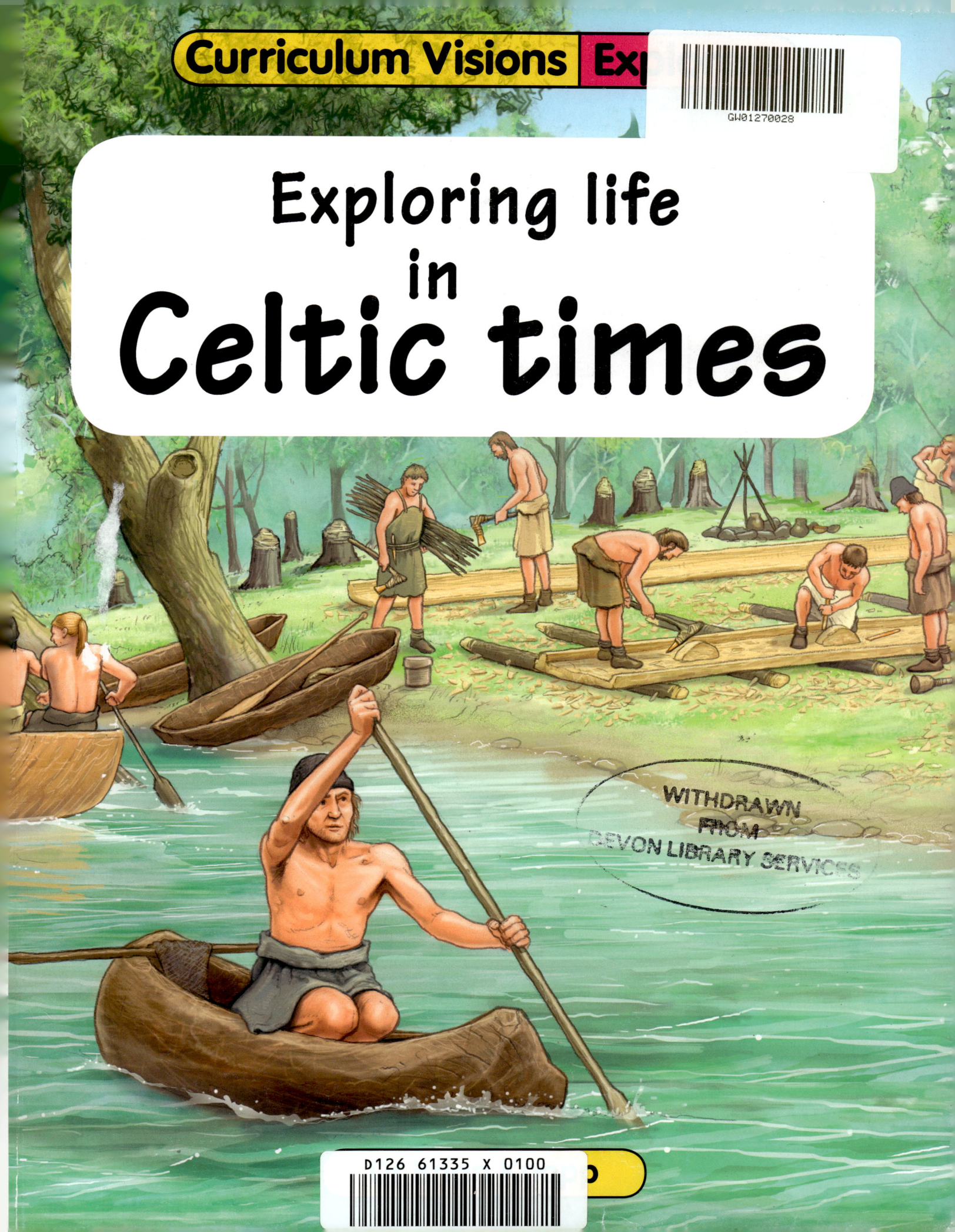

Exploring life in Celtic times

World history

First Middle East civilisations (11000BC–1268AD)

11000 BC **10000 BC** **9000 BC** **8000 BC** **7000 BC** **6000 BC** **5000 BC**

Almost everyone in Celtic times (Bronze Age and Iron Age) was a farmer. Only a very few people made bronze swords, daggers and so on. In fact, most people would have carried on using stone tools because bronze ones were expensive.

Celtic timeline

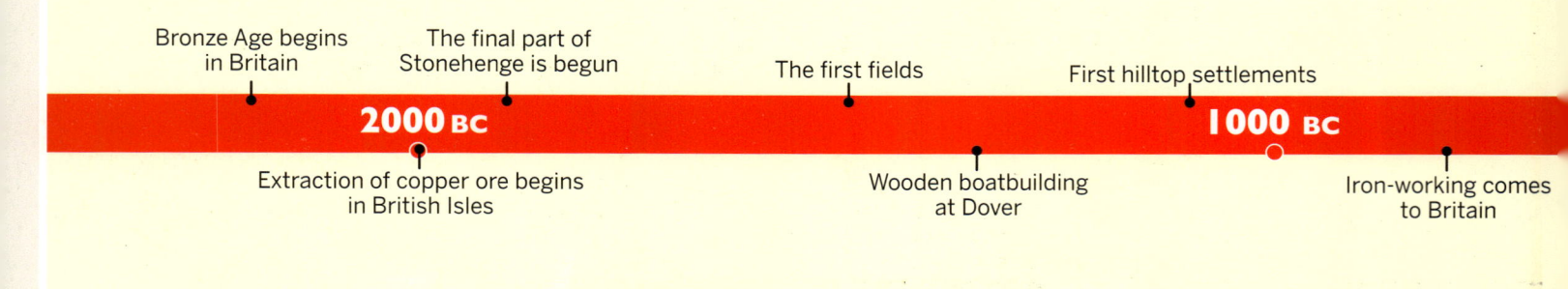

- Bronze Age begins in Britain
- The final part of Stonehenge is begun
- The first fields
- First hilltop settlements

2000 BC **1000 BC**

- Extraction of copper ore begins in British Isles
- Wooden boatbuilding at Dover
- Iron-working comes to Britain

Bronze Age

Celtic times (2200BC–440AD)

Second World War (1939–1945)

4000 BC — 3000 BC — 2000 BC — 1000 BC — 0 — 1000 AD — 2000 AD

Ancient Greeks (800–146BC)
Anglo-Saxons (450–1066)
Vikings (800–1066/1400)
Tudors (1485–1603)
Victorians (1837–1901)
Ancient Egyptians (3000–332BC)
Romans (700BC–476AD)

Contents

Were we Celts? 4
The Bronze Age 6
A land of farmers 8
A world of skills 10
Bronze Age homes 12
The Iron Age 14
Farming 16
Iron Age homes 18
Iron Age hillforts 20
An end to Celtic times 22
Glossary and index 24

Look up the **bold** words in the glossary on page 24 of this book.

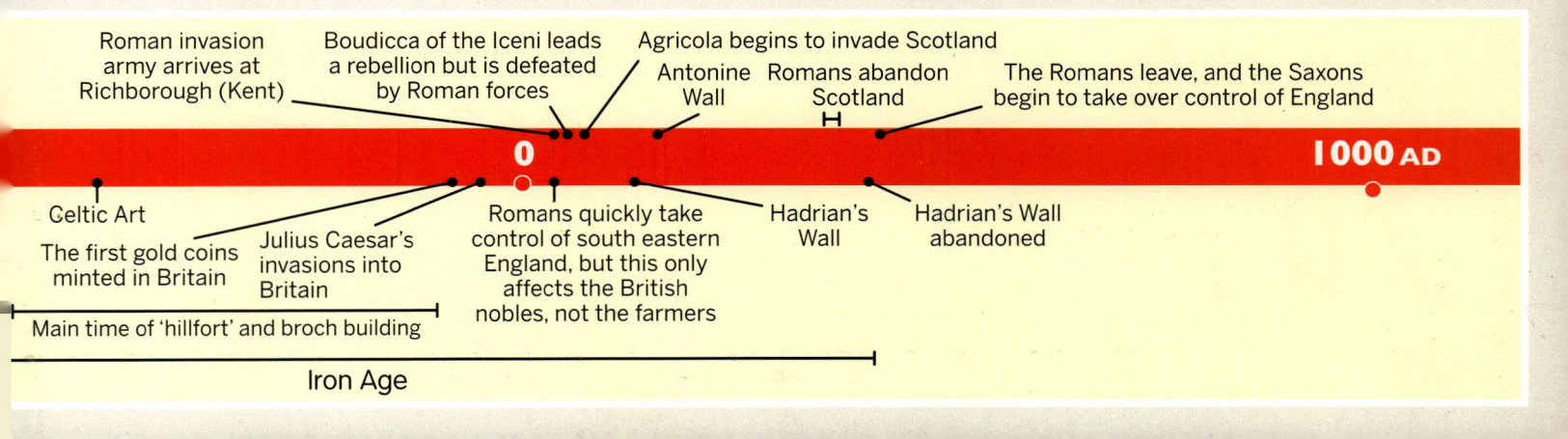

Roman invasion army arrives at Richborough (Kent)
Boudicca of the Iceni leads a rebellion but is defeated by Roman forces
Agricola begins to invade Scotland
Antonine Wall
Romans abandon Scotland
The Romans leave, and the Saxons begin to take over control of England

0 — 1000 AD

Celtic Art
The first gold coins minted in Britain
Julius Caesar's invasions into Britain
Romans quickly take control of south eastern England, but this only affects the British nobles, not the farmers
Hadrian's Wall
Hadrian's Wall abandoned

Main time of 'hillfort' and broch building

Iron Age

Were we Celts?

This is a book with the title of Celts. Celts is now a popular word to use. However, it is a modern word, first introduced in the 18th century. The people in the past did not think of themselves as Celts at all.

So what do we understand about the people we commonly call 'Celts'? They were the British – people who lived in Britain from the end of **Stone Age** times to the start of Saxon and Viking times. They are **ancestors** to most of us who live in Britain even today. That is why some other people use the words Ancient Britons.

The Stone Age finished and the Bronze Age began when people began to make tools of metal.

They used bronze because it was easy to make in a fire. Later they learned how to use a much harder metal – iron. These people lived in the Iron Age.

The Ancient Britons were very skilled, but they did not leave written records, so what we know of them comes from the writings of other people at the time – the Greeks and the Romans. But they did not call the Britons 'Celts', either.

The British and the ancient 'French', 'Spanish' and 'Germans' shared many things, like language and art, because they traded together. Some people from these areas probably came to live in western Britain, as well.

Did you know…?

- No one invaded Britain through the whole of Stone Age, Bronze Age and Iron Age times – until the Romans in 55BC.
- The people who lived in the west of Britain spoke a kind of French because they traded with the French.
- The people who lived in the south and east of Britain spoke a kind of German because they traded with the Germans.
- No one thought of themselves as Celts, or Britons, at the time because they belonged to small **tribes**, not a single country.
- Today some people think being Celtish is romantic because they like thinking of themselves as being somehow different. But the peoples of the time would not have understood this idea.

Q When was the word 'Celt' first used?

The Bronze Age

The Bronze Age gets its name from the first time people worked with bronze. Bronze is a mixture of two soft metals: copper and tin. But bronze was extremely rare and, even by the end of the Bronze Age, it was only used for valuable things such as tools and weapons. For everything else they used stone, pottery, bone and wood – just as in the Stone Age.

Because bronze was so precious, it was also used to make offerings to the gods. Many sickles, axes and swords were made just to be buried as offerings to the gods. They were never used.

Bronze hand axe

Sickles used for harvesting wheat

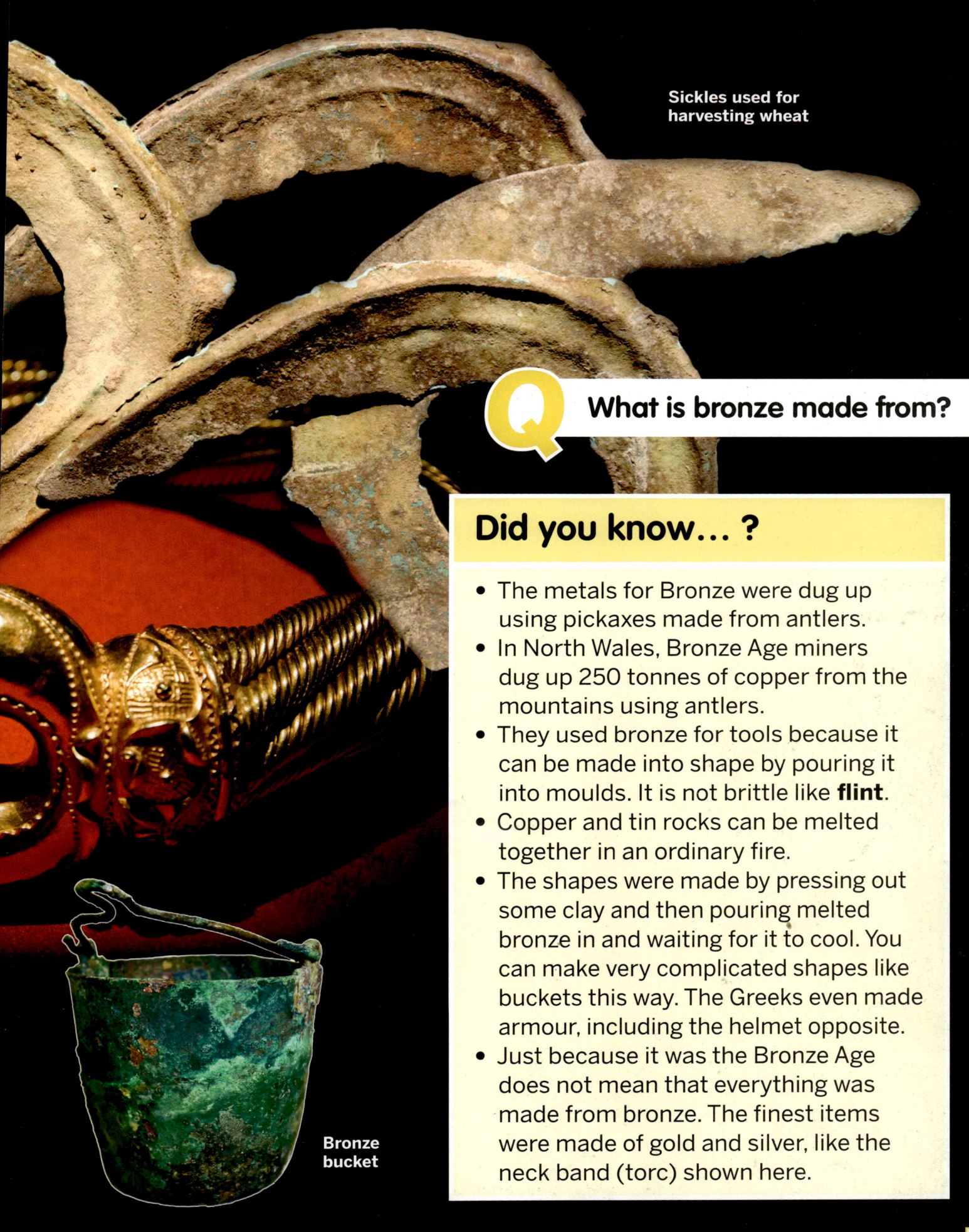

Bronze bucket

Q What is bronze made from?

Did you know… ?

- The metals for Bronze were dug up using pickaxes made from antlers.
- In North Wales, Bronze Age miners dug up 250 tonnes of copper from the mountains using antlers.
- They used bronze for tools because it can be made into shape by pouring it into moulds. It is not brittle like **flint**.
- Copper and tin rocks can be melted together in an ordinary fire.
- The shapes were made by pressing out some clay and then pouring melted bronze in and waiting for it to cool. You can make very complicated shapes like buckets this way. The Greeks even made armour, including the helmet opposite.
- Just because it was the Bronze Age does not mean that everything was made from bronze. The finest items were made of gold and silver, like the neck band (torc) shown here.

A land of farmers

Through most of the Stone Age, people were **hunter-gatherers**. They just needed some places to meet from time to time, and the stone circles gave them that. But farming changed everything. It made people stay in one place, and so great seasonal meetings were no longer possible.

Farmers also looked at the world differently from wanderers and they changed the way they thought of their gods. So they abandoned the stone circles forever. By the middle of the Bronze Age people were also making fields everywhere. Stone Age ideas were dead.

Woollen clothes and hat

Small fields with boundary banks or ditches

Did you know… ?

- Bronze Age people dug ditches, made banks, and created fields in which to keep their little animals.
- Bronze Age cows and other animals were much smaller than the ones we have today, like the brown Soay sheep.
- People started by clearing hilly land, not valleys. Valleys had wet, heavy clay soils and were difficult to use. They also chose the edges of marshes.
- They still went hunting and fishing to add meat to their diets, for there were still lots of forests about.

Antlers for hoes and ploughs

Q What were Bronze Age sheep like?

A world of skills

Early Stone Age people had made their clothes from animal skins. But by the Bronze Age people had invented spinning and weaving wool, and making clothes.

Stone Age people had traded flints. By the Bronze Age, skilled people were making clay pots for everyday use. But they also traded things made of bronze, such as axe heads, hoe heads and daggers.

Carts were used to carry things about the farm, not between places, for there were no good tracks. If people wanted to get about they used boats. One of the world's oldest seagoing boats was made in the Bronze Age. Its remains have been found near Dover. It is 15m long and 2.4m wide. The boat was made of two flat-bottom planks, four side-planks and two end-planks. The joints were stuffed with moss, wax and resin to make the boat watertight.

The boat-builders used bronze axes, chisels and gouges – they could not have made a boat like this before bronze was invented.

Loom frames were made with branches lashed up into a square. The long strands of wool were kept tight by tying little discs of stone to the lower ends. Bone needles were used to weave the thread in and out.

Q **How did Bronze Age people make clothes?**

Did you know… ?

- The first Bronze Age people used the square of wool cloth that came off the **loom**, and wrapped it around themselves. They tied it up with string or fixed it around themselves using brooches. (The Greeks were doing the same, but with cotton, as they lived in a warmer country.)
- By gouging out wood, they could make bowls, spoons and many other useful things.
- These early people did not use money. Instead they traded one kind of good with another, for example a clay pot for some wheat.
- Small wooden carts were made with solid wheels (spokes were invented later).
- Boats were made by fixing planks together. This meant they could be bigger than dug-out canoes. They made boats big enough to cross the English Channel in Bronze Age times.

11

Bronze Age homes

People did not live in small families as we do today, but as a group of related people. So they built large houses where many people could live. That was also better in case of attack. They also used homes as shelters for animals.

They needed quite a bit of space for all the family members and animals.

A typical house was 10m or so across. It was made using young tree stems for the frame. The walls were filled in with mud, straw and a dose of cattle dung. The roof was made of tree bark held in place with heavy grass turfs.

Loom

Outer circle of support posts filled in with sticks, mud, animal hair and dung

Q Who lived in a Bronze Age house?

Inner circle of posts to support the roof

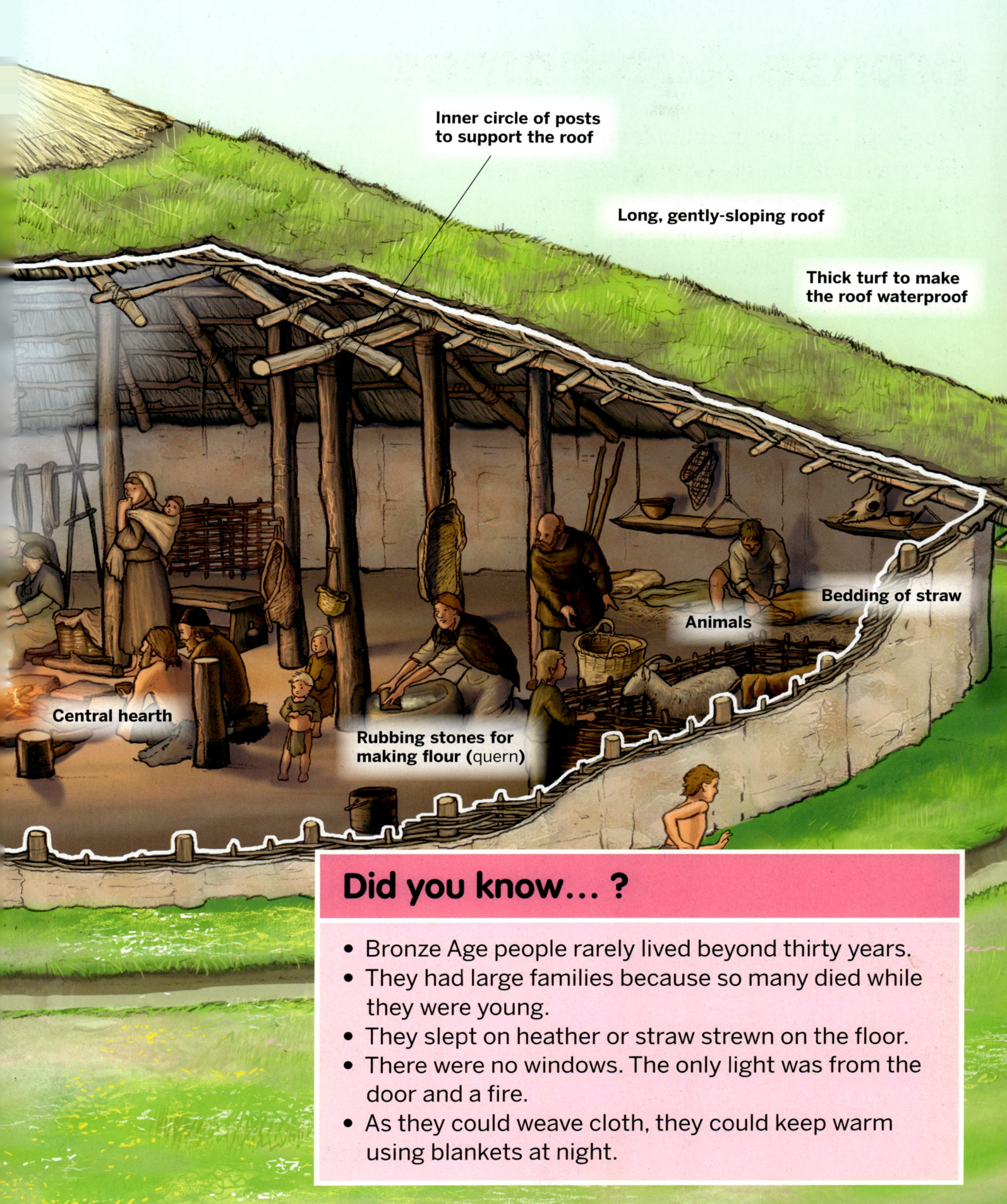

Long, gently-sloping roof

Thick turf to make the roof waterproof

Bedding of straw

Animals

Central hearth

Rubbing stones for making flour (quern)

Did you know… ?

- Bronze Age people rarely lived beyond thirty years.
- They had large families because so many died while they were young.
- They slept on heather or straw strewn on the floor.
- There were no windows. The only light was from the door and a fire.
- As they could weave cloth, they could keep warm using blankets at night.

The Iron Age

Iron is much harder to make and to use than bronze. You need a **furnace**, not an ordinary open fire.

Iron is harder and tougher than bronze. Sword blades take a better edge; the tips of ploughs last longer when made of iron instead of bronze.

But no-one used iron unless it was really important to do so, because it was difficult to make. Most people still used wood, stone and a little bronze for their day-to-day needs.

Iron Age Britons never built any great cities like the Greeks or Romans. This is probably because they lived where the land almost everywhere was good for farming, and trade was less important. They wrote down nothing about their way of life either. The Romans and Greeks, on the other hand, developed writing skills. As a result it was they who wrote about the ancient Britons, not the British.

In the Scottish mountains people lived in small communities where they could find patches of fertile land. They built tower houses, like little castles. They called them brochs.

This sword uses iron for the blade because iron is stronger and will take a sharper edge, but bronze is used for the handle because bronze can be made into a more complicated shape.

Did you know…?

- Iron was first used in what is now Turkey about a thousand years before people in Britain learned how to use it.
- The Iron Age in Britain started about 800BC, when the knowledge of how to use iron reached Britain.
- Most people got joint diseases from hard work.
- Men wore woollen or linen shirts and trousers, and women wore blouses, dresses or skirts. During the winter men wore cloaks, and women wore shawls. Many wore a neckband (torc) all their lives.

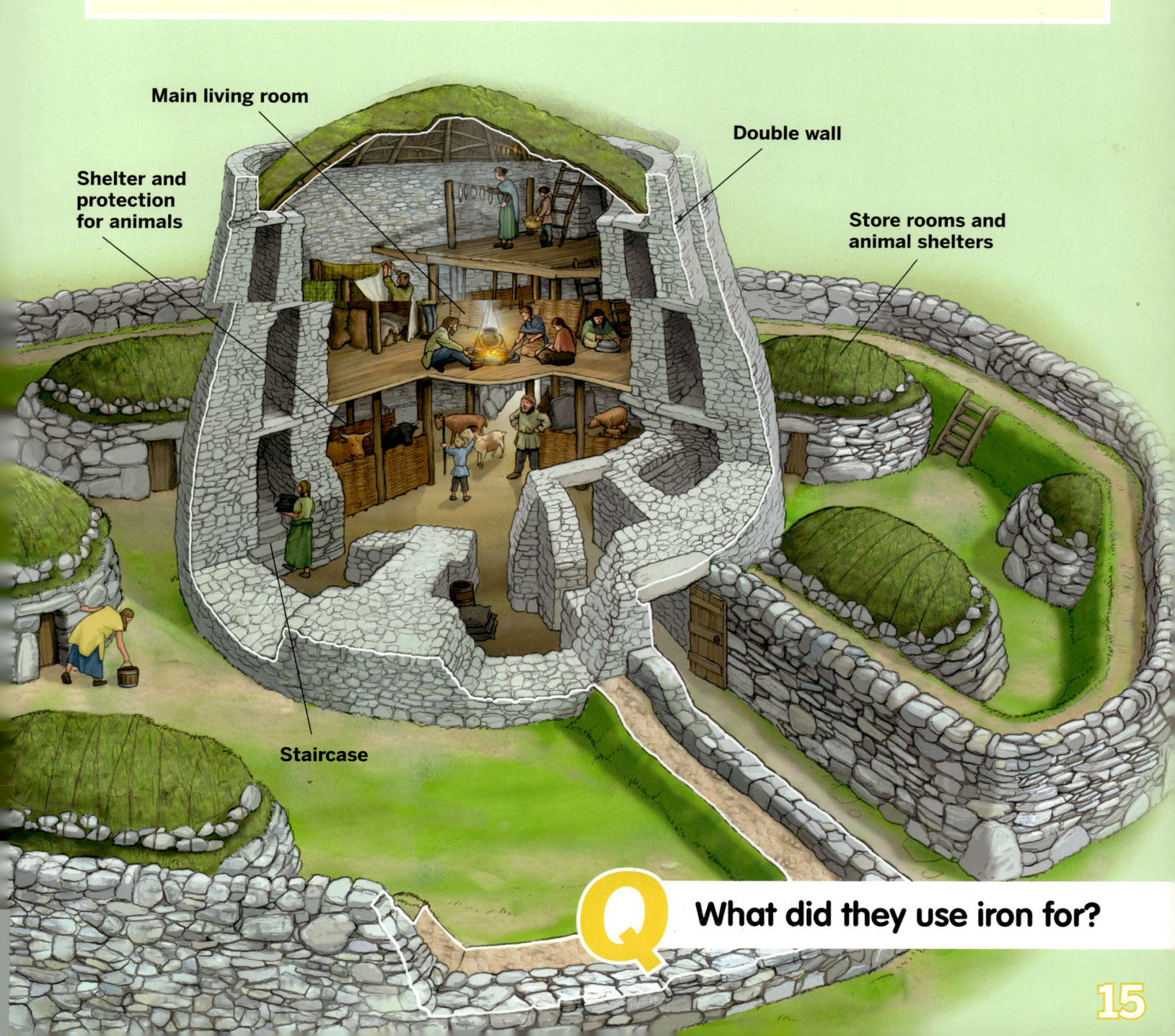

Main living room

Double wall

Shelter and protection for animals

Store rooms and animal shelters

Staircase

Q What did they use iron for?

Sowing seeds was done by broadcasting them (scattering them by the handful)

Weeds had to be hoed out and birds kept at bay

Did you know…?

- Farmers did not sit around and do nothing at night. Most people made clothes by weaving them by firelight.
- In some places people farmed on slopes because the land was easier to clear than in valley bottoms. As they ploughed, so some of the soil moved downslope. The farmers used this effect to make wide benches, or terraces, across the hillsides. They are known as 'lynchets'.
- Timber was a crop, for wood was needed to make almost everything. Many trees were coppiced (cut close to the ground) because this produced lots of sturdy straight, flexible shoots that were ideal for building with.
- In some places, such as near the sea, there was the chance to get salt from seawater and trade it. Those near clay made pots, those near copper and iron were part-time miners, and so on.

Q What name would we now use instead of lynchet?

Flat strip of land produced by ploughing across the slope

Iron-tipped plough

Farming

Almost everyone in Iron Age Britain was a farmer. Most people – including craftsmen and even warriors – would have lived in a farm or small farming village. Farmers had to spend almost all of their time farming just to feed their families.

Most farmers grew wheat and barley, and kept cattle, sheep and pigs. But new crops, animals, tools and ideas gradually spread from Europe. Beans, cats and chickens were all introduced to British Iron Age farmers.

Iron Age homes

By Iron Age times, homes were smaller and had steeper roofs. They were surrounded by fences to keep wild animals out, but inside they were still a mix of living space for people, night-time protection for animals and a place for storing grain. In the centre of the house was the open fire. It was used for giving heat and light as well as for cooking food. There were no windows.

Conical roof of stout timbers supported by stone walls or timbers filled with sticks and mud depending on what was available

Thorn fence to enclose the house

Doorway

Thatched roof

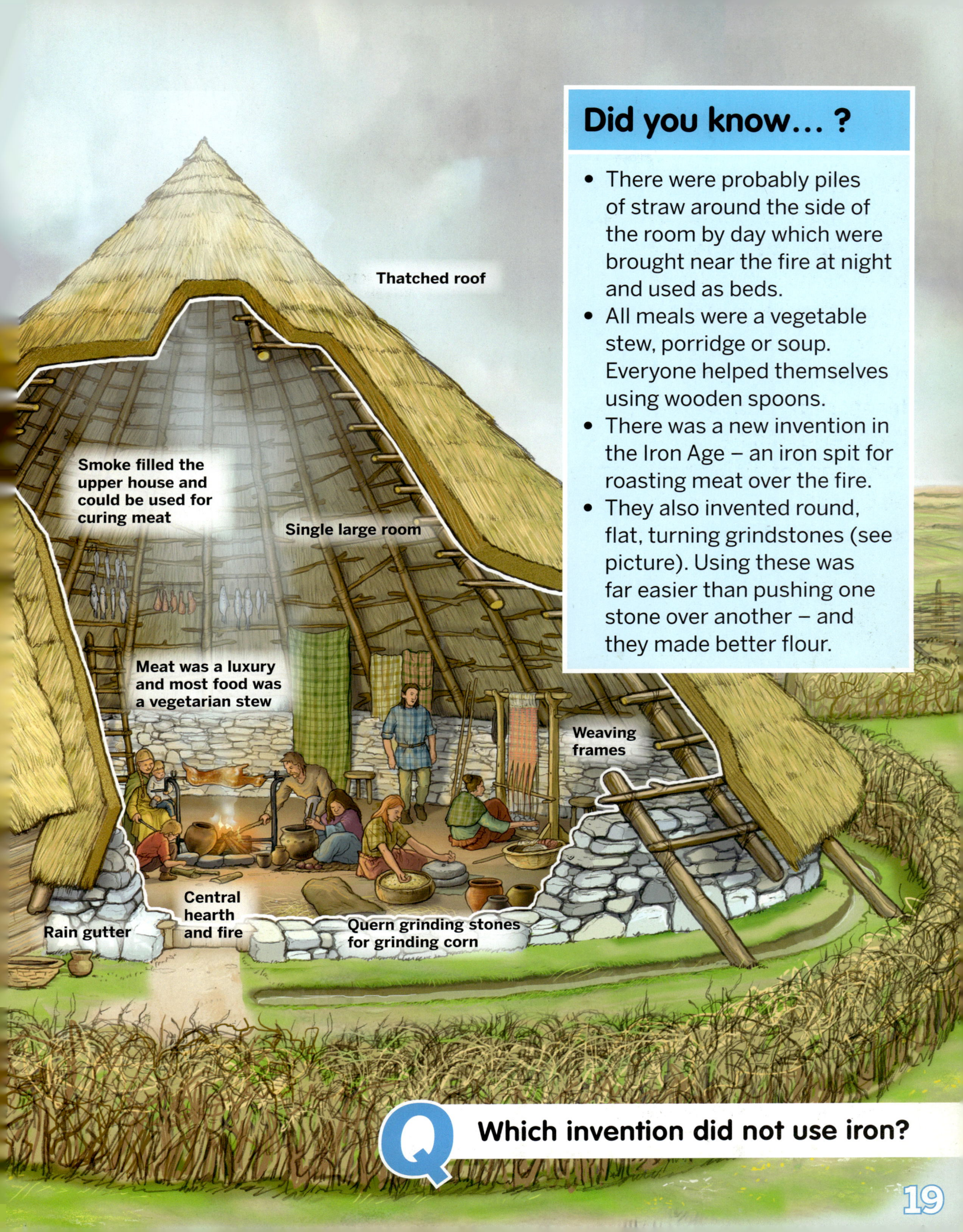

Smoke filled the upper house and could be used for curing meat

Single large room

Meat was a luxury and most food was a vegetarian stew

Weaving frames

Rain gutter

Central hearth and fire

Quern grinding stones for grinding corn

Did you know… ?

- There were probably piles of straw around the side of the room by day which were brought near the fire at night and used as beds.
- All meals were a vegetable stew, porridge or soup. Everyone helped themselves using wooden spoons.
- There was a new invention in the Iron Age – an iron spit for roasting meat over the fire.
- They also invented round, flat, turning grindstones (see picture). Using these was far easier than pushing one stone over another – and they made better flour.

Q Which invention did not use iron?

Did you know… ?

- Most people lived in the lowlands nearby, not in the hillforts.
- The top of the uppermost ridge was finished off with pointed stakes to stop it being overrun by invaders.
- The forts had room for plenty of food, but there is no sign they had wells, so the defenders could not have held out against an attacker for long. That is why, when the Romans arrived, they simply lay **siege** to the forts.
- The centre of the fort may have been used as a **shrine** to the British gods.

Iron Age hillforts

During the Iron Age, the number of people increased, and the tribes became organised into kingdoms.

It was at this time that people started to worry about defending their lands and goods. This is when they began to build great hilltop 'forts' – rings of ditches and banks.

As attacks were rare, it is likely these hilltop sites were built for storing grain and possibly for worship. Grain was, after all, the most precious thing they had.

Forts might also have been a sign of power – just as palaces were built by kings in later ages to show how important they were.

The entrance paths into hillforts were built in a 'dog's leg' pattern so that attackers could not charge directly at the gate.

Q What was the centre of the fort used for?

An end to Celtic times

The Romans arrived in Britain because their general, Julius Caesar, decided to **conquer** more land.

The British warriors were not full-time soldiers. They only fought when they had to. As a result, they were no match for the well-trained and full-time Roman army. Within a century of the first invasion Britain was a part of the Roman Empire and called Britannia.

Roman invasion

When the Romans arrived there were two million British. During Roman times the British still farmed the land and ruled their little kingdoms. Sometimes they rebelled, as when Queen Boudicca led the Iceni tribe on a rampage. But they could never beat the Romans. Instead, they relied on the Romans to keep invaders away. When the Romans left in 410 AD, the British could not protect themselves from the Saxons and Angles who sailed over and raided from Germany.

But the new 'invaders' could not kill off all of these people or force them to flee westwards. The Britons survived. But much about their way of life and language did not. They simply became part of the Saxon lands, and gradually blended in to Saxon life, while their villages got new names – Saxon names.

Did you know… ?

- Britons went in to battle wearing war paint (blue dye made from woad). Some British warriors thought they were more frightening when they were naked.
- Their way of fighting was to stand in front of the opposing army and scream and beat their spears and swords against their shields. They then ran headlong into the opposing army, screaming the entire way. It was meant to scare off the other army. It did not work with the Romans.

Saxon attackers

Q **What happened to the Ancient Britons?**

Glossary

ancestor
A relative who lived a long time ago.

conquer
To defeat a group of people and take over their land.

flint
A type of stone that can be broken into pieces with sharp edges.

furnace
A very hot fire used to melt metals.

hunter-gatherer
A person who gets food by hunting animals and gathering edible plants.

loom
A frame used for weaving.

quern
A pair of stones used for hand-grinding corn to make flour.

shrine
A place where people put offerings to their god(s).

siege
When attackers surround an area and do not let people or supplies come in or out.

Stone Age
The time when people started using stone tools. It came before the Bronze Age.

tribe
A group of related people who live and work together.

Index

ancestors 4, 24
boat 10-11
Boudicca, Queen 23
bronze 4, 6-7, 10, 14
conquer 22, 24
farming 8-9, 14, 16-17, 23
flint 7, 10, 24
food 9, 17, 18-19, 20-21
furnace 14, 24
Greeks 4, 7, 11, 14
hillfort 20-21
hunter-gatherers 8, 24
home/house/household 12-13, 18-19
iron 4, 14-15, 16
invasion 5, 20-21, 22-23
loom 11, 24
metals 4, 6-7, 14-15, 16
mould 7
rebel 23
quern 13, 19, 24
Romans 4, 5, 14, 20, 22-23
Saxon 4, 23
shrine 20, 24
siege 20, 24
Stone Age 4, 6, 8, 10
stone circle 8
tools 4, 6-7, 10-11, 16-17, 19
trade 4-5, 10-11, 14, 16
tribe 5, 21, 24
weapons 6, 10, 14, 23
weaving/clothing 10-11, 13, 15, 16
wood 23

Curriculum Visions

Curriculum Visions Explorers
This series provides straightforward introductions to key worlds and ideas.

You might also be interested in
Our slightly more detailed book, Celtic times, and others such as Exploring the first civilisations, The Stone Age, The ancient Egyptians, The ancient Greeks, The Romans in Britain and Ancient Rome.

www.CurriculumVisions.com
(Subscription required)

© Atlantic Europe Publishing 2014

First reprint 2014.

The right of Brian Knapp to be identified as the author of this work has been asserted by him in accordance with the Copyright, Designs and Patents Act 1988.

All rights reserved. No part of this publication may be reproduced, stored in a retrieval system, or transmitted in any form or by any means, electronic, mechanical, photocopying, recording or otherwise, without prior permission of the copyright holder.

Author
Brian Knapp, BSc, PhD
Senior Designer
Adele Humphries, BA, PGCE
Editors
Gillian Gatehouse
Emily Pulsford, BA
Illustrations
Mark Stacey
Designed and produced by
Atlantic Europe Publishing
Printed in China by
WKT Company Ltd

Exploring life in Celtic times – Curriculum Visions
A CIP record for this book is available from the British Library.
Paperback ISBN 978 1 78278 076 2

Picture credits
All photographs are from the Earthscape and ShutterStock Picture Libraries.

This product is manufactured from sustainable managed forests. For every tree cut down at least one more is planted.